My Manifold City

Acknowledgements
Some of the poems in this collection were printed in
*Cyphers, The Literary Review, The New Hungarian Quarterly
Numbers, The Rialto, Visions* and *Webster Review,* as well as in the
anthologies *The Windless Orchard, Homage to Mandelstam* and
Klaonica. Nine of the poems in this collection were also included in the
anthology *If . . .* (The Starwheel Press with the
Cheltenham Festival of Literature, 1991).

First published in 1996 by
The Alba Press
46 Grantchester Road
Cambridge CB3 9ED

ISBN 0 9527605 0 9

Printed in Hungary by Argumentum Publishing and Printing House (Budapest)

George Gömöri

My Manifold City

Poems
*translated from Hungarian
by Clive Wilmer and the author*

The Alba Press

For Beata, Anna, Daniel, Peter and Bence

Contents

My Manifold City

Poems 1958-1995

Translated by Clive Wilmer and the author with the exception of
"Lazarus" (Tony Connor) and "Christmas 1956" (George Szirtes)

On a Dawn Road

As I set out at six in the morning on the Dumfries road from Stranraer
with the smoke-swirls of the Celtic sky above, it chanced that I passed
along by the sea which, child-like, smiled sweetly in its sleep –
and yellow bushes at the roadside were aroused with tiny noises
and even the wind awoke in a pink mood, clapping its hands –
then, suddenly, I felt the twinge of my unslept Budapest dawns,
those raw, dazed, shivering dawns, of my ripening years,
and I felt as if again I were walking on empty streets, the patter
of my footsteps answering a dry broom's crack and scratch,
the first tram of the day with a screech turned into the corner
and, tasting of blood and salt, a wind blew from the Danube . . .
My memories fade as gaslamps fade at daybreak,
but my faithless loyalty will last out my life –
dreaming of Budapest dawns, I walk down the Dumfries road
and know that what awaits me at the end of the road is home.

Miracle in Manhattan

In the whole of New York what I liked best
was the tree: that tree with its dense foliage
spreading its arms up there on the roof,
green and abandoned as the everyday miracle
that is the created world.
Life round about it was choked with concrete,
a jungle of bricks entangled everything,
and by night the tree there called to mind
a lone sentry, intently watching,
who stands his ground for us. In the street's depth,
a muddled age keeps droning, teeming by,
while the tree stands fifteen storeys up
and lives, and keeps on living,
above and beyond the racing of machines.
You should live this way too, for the future's sake,
with all the beauty and courage of that tree,
shaping the light that falls on you into colours,
that the melody of life might blossom skyward.

Expectant Mother

I am cold. All the time the foetus
has been in my womb I've felt the cold.
I see the world through glass, from under water.
He can't grasp this, the man I call
husband. He thinks he's superfluous.
I can't share my joy with him
and there are no words to express my pain.
I await the Sixth Day anxiously;
how much can happen by then, oh God!
In the dream, my doctor brings flaming roses,
he whispers in my ear that he loves me only.
We elope at night-time, our gondola sways.

Restless March

This is the time of waiting.
Of heavy nights, tossing and turning in bed.
Is it the hot wind tearing at taut cables
or the touch of cramped time
that makes our nerves bristle and quiver?

I can't say. The future wears
a compassionate Boddhisatva smile.
When the lava stops flowing
the village folk (fresh victims are needed all the time)
return to plant the rice.

– Hope, what an inexhaustible cornucopia
you are! what an eternal obsession!

Once the earth was quaking under my feet.
I have seen a rain of ashes, and I know:
sometimes our life is weighed in a single word.

There is a time for thanksgiving,
and a time for sacrifice.
Now each day resounds like a gong.
This is the time of waiting:

a time growing full like the moon.

Lazarus

Lazarus lies on his deathbed,
resisting the end, unwilling to die.

He trusts in resurrection, yet he doesn't;
he longs for immortality,
but the spell of the transient still binds his limbs.

Now he recalls the green smell of marshy meadows,
the nestling warmth of women's flesh
and cool flute-notes in the evening.

Then his sigh blows out the candle's splutter,
five seals are set on his unwritten farewell letter.
He sleeps, and in a nightmare sees the Spirit
mould Adam from dust – and all that we inherit.

These are the agonies of voluntary death.
The pains the living cannot imagine.

A great stone is rolled into his tomb's mouth –
but it will not stop the miracle to come
when lo! dead Lazarus walks out on the third day,
and looks into the never-closing eyes of God.

Found Images

Cherubim sing in the splendour of a shelled egg
which gleams like the Arctic sun.

A pink submarine glow,
fruit rocking in a coral-bay –
once plucked it will dry with shrill cries.

Sea-shells, pebbles, round stones and crags,
and the sea roars, in a naked ear, faintly.

Marilyn's arching back, her amber necklace,
on her face the bewildered smile of a falling tea-rose.

And finally: a harshly cracked landscape.
Brown limbs, grey earth, awaiting the rain's lash.

Mandelshtam in Exile

Our living space, all measured out,
Our days are numbered, one and all;
Through the steppe's silver night, you hear
A wolf, haggard and starving, howl.

This is a dead, inhuman land
Whose power no god or demon wields.
The glimmer of the Arctic light
Is the far smile of crystal worlds.

The blood-stained star of destiny
Has set out on its path through space;
There are no saving miracles –
Nor can remorse now win you grace.

There's no one to deflect the track
Of the knives whistling straight for you.
Persephone, standing at your back,
Proffers her hand. Hold yours out too.

Letter from a Declining Empire

Ever more frightening, ever more rapacious,
barbarian incursions are troubling
the Empire of Autumn. And galloping on, the northerly wind
screeches through cloud-crevices, shears off
leafy crowns, tears down
beech-tree robes the colour of sealing-wax,
shedding their heavy blood,
cracking its whip at defencelessly shuddering maples –
and how the gold coins keep falling!
Down threadbare avenues, past gap-toothed palings
the raider's clattering by; he throws
a firebrand into a chestnut-tree, and whoosh!
leaves whirl and fly up into
an air-woven hoop of flame. There's no one by
to save the treasures, the infidel
can pillage unhindered, now only
the scattered watchtowers of silver fir are left standing.
And still the conquest is not complete. In vain
do frost-riders patrol down by the river,
in vain does the Khan exact ransom from the milder
October colours, from sky-blue and green;
the survivors learn how to live. Naked as
cornstalks rent and torn, and with earth's bitterness.
Once the marauders have cleared off, their savage
symbols will melt too trickling down the gardens, and then
of a sudden the new
but eternal year will rise and raise with sunshine a still
more beautiful empire.

From a Traveller's Notebook

In Ruritania
there are no plugs in the baths
lavatory seats aren't sat upon but vomited over
offices smell of cabbage
culture of cheap eau de Cologne
With thickly padded shoulders in a jacket cut too straight
the writer stalks about in the field of Word
he bends down picks up a piece of reality
sniffs at it and chucks it away grimacing
he makes a bouquet of dew-drenched immortelles
for his fadeless merits
he shall while he lives be exalted
in Ruritania
the job of ceremonial incense-bearer
is not for everyone
only for those whose past *and* future
are equally beyond reproach
the dispensation of incense is important
though it does not make the task of post-perfuming
any less necessary
In the shops there is a crowd
for it is rumoured that a large consignment
of word-stock has arrived
words beginning with 'x' are on sale again
and there are 'z'-s galore (or so they say)
Oooh and if plugs should appear at last
sheets of sandpaper and pastry cutters
then in Ruritania
the deluge of satisfaction would shatter everything

Young Writer in Eastern Europe

Can one who looks toward more distant things,
slip free of the iron ring that is mere chance?
Everywhere are the same old booby-traps,
the same barbed-wire entanglements,
the same elusive enemy,
mine-throwers disguised by protective colouring,
and even on each horizon the same hillocks,
their colours indefinable,
with flowers that may or may not possess
a vague odour.

To live differently. One could, perhaps . . . but how?
Instead of indeterminate boundaries
the mind needs a magnetic field,
instead of the odd chance, certainty
(weather conditions notwithstanding).
There is nothing to pour out with the bath water,
and how do you lie on a bed made by another?
Not much remains: black anecdotes, maxims,
occasional pieces done for the media. Taped music
wafting faintly through rooms with the curtains drawn
and love made to nameless girls.

Data for a Natural History
of Small Nations

Small Nations
as a rule peep out of the pockets of big ones
and there they rave and wave their arms about:
'vile usurper!'
or
'dearest friend!'
at times of historic hurricanes
they fall into hoof-prints brimming with water
heavy cavalry clatters over them
they are rolled flat by caterpillar tracks
but those who survive
tattered and torn maimed and half-paralysed
go on raving and waving –
in disbelief the giants shake their heads:
'what resilience!'
'who would have believed it?'

these small nations can take quite a lot

Memories of a Train Journey

Beer bottles, lemonade bottles, their rhythmical clink,
bread-crusts, green pepper cores in a plastic bag;
a cheap novel – *Wyatt Earp: Hero*
of the Wild West (to be continued), dog-eared;
a rust spot left on the blue plush by a fag-end,
ashtrays Pompeian in their abundance, dead matchsticks,
reading-lamps wrenched from their sockets,
sporting chronicles, several days old, in shreds; the smell
of excrement, soot, clouds of stale sweat
that the finest fibre, the viscera of the carriage
were permeated with. Cultures of dirt.
And something that has no palpable trace, the hope-
less tossing and turning, the whining, the curses
muttered and mumbled as if in prayer, because
you've just got to live like this, like a stray dog,
just shuttled back and forth between no fixed stations.

A Situation

he who lives across from a watchtower
he whose window looks out onto a gaol
will not be dazzled by vain hopes
will not be seduced by sham perspectives

travelling does not tempt him either
for he knows: there is no way out –
from here a road leads into the clouds
built out of paper, stones and sweat

he comes finally into a haven
the bay and the shores of family beckon
and as he writes his memoirs and goes ga-ga
it's only his past that hums like a samovar

Island in the Mediterranean

Nothing is impossible on this island:
Calypso might just be the name of a boat
as much as a nymph. As for the sea,
not wine-dark, it's more of a blue or green,
gentian, or several shades of amethyst.
But there is, as the tale has it in H.,
'poplar and alder and fragrant cypress'
and a monastery garden full of amphoras.
Odysseus, under a wine-trellis,
drinks wine; he does not brood on the shore.
Seven days – not years – soon pass, no, run:
an occasion for tears. By night the cave's
redolent of parsley, no irises here –
they've withered – just aloes and oleanders
and endless fields of flowering lavender.
The past grinds down the Trojan hecatomb
and only the gods can see that he'll make it home.
Not for him immortality, for he of the gods' sweet
idyll desires no part but, glad to have found love, he wave-like
mounts and again comes to rest in Calypso's arms now,
                                        the wanderer.

Abda

In memory of Miklós Radnóti*

They made us dig. Leaden, grey,
the sky is empty of all but the beat –
exhausted, slow – of a rook's wings.
Carts over there, bored soldiers.
(How banal it is, the entire setting!)
And these aren't even Germans.
We speak the same language and yet the guard
can't understand a word I say.
The Book's prophecy and that of my own
prophetic soul are proving true.
The sponge is dipped in vinegar.
I pocket the little notebook now,
still inhaling the pasture's damp
and the brushwood smoke that wreathes the willows.
Non omnis moriar – yes I know,
but now for the last time I can say *I am*:
I shall be a flame that soars in the broad sky,
a silent body laid in the damp earth.

*Hungarian poet of Jewish origin, killed in 1944 at the age
of 35, near the village of Abda in Hungary. He was buried
in a mass grave; his body was identified at the
exhumation in 1946 by a notebook of poems found in the
pocket of his raincoat.*

Notes on Lindbergh

Lindbergh crossed the Atlantic by air
in 1927. At take-off eight people
pushed his plane – the propeller also
had to be started manually. Over New-
foundland he got lost in the fog for a moment but,
once it cleared, he started out on that long stretch of
hitherto invincible water. And he crossed it.
My mother was in Paris at the time; she never
learned how to sew properly, it is true, but she did return
with some fabulous Chevalier numbers, and she still sometimes
cooks French beans as the French do. Lindbergh
was the sensation of the hour – not without luck,
for though his wings got packed with ice, it melted
nonetheless in time. When the compass
stopped working, L. watched the stars
correcting his course by them.
Now and then he had a nap but he always
managed to wake in time. At Le Bourget
a crowd of 200,000 was awaiting him, they rushed
towards him yelling: 'Lind-ber! Lind-ber!'
Not unlike *another* yelling, heard
only a few years later: 'Sieg-heil! Sieg-heil!'
Yes. Because later this handsome pilot,
who was naive, far too naive, came out on the side of
non-intervention (read Hitler), for which the Germans
gave him a medal . . . You can tell a bird
by its feathers. But in 1927 he was as yet
the youngest son, the hero of tales,
who could do what no one else had done before him.
Lindbergh . . . and what happened to his baby?
The world had hailed him but that was no help:
the baby vanished, never to be found.
It's an old truth but it's useful: be a hero,
an anxious father, a political fall-guy, you cannot
avoid your fate – beg pardon – I mean your roles.

A Phantastic Topography

"A desert country near the sea"
                                Shakespeare

where screws and assistant caretakers
teach philosophy
there the philosophers
become night watchmen at the Zoo
where the state has reason to be afraid
of Aristotle
there objective reality has come to an end
under the sky of an addled myth
even informers scurry about in jeans
under a sky with knitted brows
raw future is the food of termite years

At Times Like This

towards the end of October
when the huge chestnut spreading its branches
majestically at the gates of King's College
turns to the colour of clear honey
and the medlar decks itself out in shades of copper
and the small fig bares its branches
no longer concealing the slightness of its yield
at times like this at the turn of autumn
I hear once again the bugle-call
sounding from far away
just moments before the parade
and the most abandoned carnival in our history
began

The Contradiction Resolved

Our habits – they're so many dragon's eggs.
Disturbed mornings, unsettled, harassed days
kindle my indignation, feeding it:
isn't it scandalous that *you*'re not *me*?
And if *I'm* not *you* – how can we stand each other?
All our things are stamped with otherness.
In bed, when I reach towards you and you kiss me,
We both suspend the negation left unspoken,
And join like the twin shells clamped round a pearl.
(So otherness after all is worth accepting.)
Of what I am, then, be the better part.

Yes, No

An old man so it's hard for him to remember
yes he was always a law-abiding man
no it wasn't the kind of work he liked
yes but then that was his job
no he was never idle at the workplace
yes the State demanded it
no he never slapped anybody's face
yes beating was forbidden in the regulations
no later on he never gave much thought to it
yes at night they drank and played cards
no he has never felt any racial hatred
yes   well what else   just an average sort of person

but orders are orders are orders are ORDERS

the final sum is 250,000 (people)
but it may be more
or less

as you get older you start forgetting
nicht wahr?

* *

why bother about details
once upon a time there was
once there was a little Polish village
Sobibor

Aerial View of a Developing Country

Something that wars (in these parts
everyday events) could not achieve
is now realized: huge craters mined-out,
half-demolished hills,
constantly smouldering rubbish-tips,
scrapheaps of ancient factories,
the most modern machines rusting in silent rain,
air polluted with special care
(for each square inch each labourer
can claim as much as a pound of dust!)
and the mild water of the lake which, at best,
gives you dysentery.
This is where we stand and I haven't yet mentioned
the clouds of lead billowing from exhausts,
the theoretical sewage-works and the much-guaranteed
nuclear plants (as to their safety you may swear to it
provided the courts don't object to perjury).
Let's not wait till the next earthquake:
if nature won't do it, man's sure
to do his utmost to create a country
where life is no longer worth living.

Gloss on Nadezhda*

'And what is it makes you think you should be happy?'
asked Osip of Nadezhda. They had, though,
some happy hours, some moments, but many more
were drenched in fear as gauze in thick blood.
Osip paid for poetry with his life; Nadezhda
spent hers embalming the frail body of lyric,
and uplifting it, tearfully. But as a French visitor
in '77 put it, "What after all can one expect from this country?"
Nadezhda's hopes were modest: to go as one came –
in bed, among pillows. Not in 50 below zero.
She expected no miracles: maybe an earthquake will raise
the seemingly dead, but peonies won't grow on the steppe,
neither will gladioli sprout from cement; dulled minds
will be dulled further with vodka, and as for the young,
they almost wish for the *Thrilling Thirties* again,
when the butcher state, smooth-fronted and muscular,
still looked out confidently towards the future: the state
which struck all other opinions,
all private beliefs and private lives stone dead,
which boiled the plentiful bones of peasant millions
in its vast cauldron – for its wretchedly meagre soup.

*Wife of Russian poet Osip Mandelshtam and author of the memoirs *Hope Against Hope*.

The Man from Nazareth

Eight hundred crucified Jews
scream from the torn scrolls –
their families massacred before their eyes, cut down,
trampled on by the victor's executioners.
What, compared to Alexander Yannaios,
was Herod the Great? A bungling child-murderer.
True, his own children were among those he murdered. But
numerically speaking? And then, compared to him,
what of Antipas, King of Galilee? And during
his tepid reign, what of the gentle fool
who was hauled before P. Pilate, the one accused
of 'sorcery' and of 'aspiring to power'?
A wild dove fluttering in the fire-storm.
And on the other hand:
a small fir-cone a forest will grow from,
a cool spring, miraculous water
to quench the thirst of millions who struggle in the desert
of history. And a face so touchingly *human*
we cannot turn our eyes away from it.

Christmas 1956

At this stage we suspect and yet should know
there's no way back. The papers paint a bleak
deserted city where sporadic rifles
rattle against a snow swaddled night.
Here Regent Street is one vast jeweller's
and 'Silent Night' spills tinsel on bright pavements.
We are invited, Andris and I, to Epping,
to an English family. We're greeted with
a crackling fire, roast turkey, and an ancient
pudding like a shrunken head (preserved
in brandy, edible). We dance in the vague darkness,
embrace the shapely daughters of the house
(but sleep with rubber bottles, not with them.)
Back home there are no mass arrests as yet,
the writers' union functions, but omens are bad,
not knowing (though suspecting) what may follow:
in our case Oxford, for friends who stayed behind
the well known prisons, semi-skilled employment;
a dark low Christmas this, the last we spend
(or even partly spend) in Hungary.

My Manifold City

My manifold city, I summon up
your image through the lenses of the seasons.
Trudging to school (in short trousers)
down an alley white with hoar-frost, when
a small bird hops over a frozen puddle:
A-B-A-B, and look, I've got a poem.
Spring: riverside kisses drowned in sighs,
buds exploding in the Museum Gardens.
Then sultry summertime, on the Island roses
surrounding me with fragrance there, and love
is unexpected fireworks on Gellért Hill.
And finally – autumn, autumn. Winged songs
arching to clear skies, flapping flags
holed in the middle, the bright hopes machine-gunned,
and the darkly gaping hollows of ruined buildings
in heavy rain that blends all into grey.

Food for the Dead

In some parts of Europe still
it's the custom to feed the dead –
the dead man's favourite dishes
in a pot or canister or simply on a plate
are set beside the grave
It is summer 1990 Once again
a restless early summer now
and a spectacular feeding time for the dead
the erstwhile Titan of the Carpathians eats his fill
of the young their flesh their broken bones
and then instead of a brandy he slurps at
gipsy blood and the blood of bearded protesters
he keeps coming back from the grave snarling
a black zombie hoarsely demanding: Food
more food more of it let me eat

The Guinea-Pig's Dilemma

The guinea-pig wakes.
He feels restless. He twitches his nose and ears –
all in one piece and the wire's no longer
sticking out of his head. There's plenty of food.
And where's the technician? Gone.
And no, it can't be true, but even the cage
has been left open. The little beast gets up,
walks round, sniffs the air and is still scared.
So has it all come to an end there – at long last?
He won't be observed any more, or poked with needles?
What was the whole thing for?
And what, now, should he do with himself?
Where should he go? Whimpering, anguished,
he feels himself gripped by a fear different in *kind*.

Present for Anna

who knows what is made in heaven –
though it was in the sky that my daughter was proposed to
in the crowded basket of a polychrome balloon
as it flew high over England
pleasant her green meadows and yellow fields

afterwards they drank on it in a pub
at the sign of the dove and rainbow
in the dove's beak perhaps an olive-branch
with the rainbow the pledge of golden peace

– we will love each other forever now, won't we?
it's a question you can't answer
but when the sky (as it often does) turns dark and when
                                                    the gale
makes doors and windows rattle in its black fury
and when the hail pours down

remember that blessed summer day
and with it the lightness of the hot-air balloon

Portrait of a Scientist

miracles still occur
in this ever more calculable world

for instance a man struck down
by a wasting disease and forced
to live in a wheelchair a man
unable to talk
(and he breathes through a valve)
a man who cannot move more
than two fingers of one hand

a brain of demonic power and two thin fingers
TALKING in a synthetic voice

the human wreck of a genius
who calculates the unimaginable
sees back to the beginning of the Cosmos
and denies the existence of God

* *

As for God
(Let's face it, a *singularity*)
He does not deny him
the right to deny

Autumn Monologue

The tart sweetness of apples nipped by frost
is what I praise now, when through the crystalline
air of this languid autumn (from time to time
tainted by smoke from bonfires of dead leaves)
I think I can hear the honking of wild fowl
and, if a light breeze makes the curtain flap,
the motorway's unbroken muted hum –
it's the tart sweetness of apples nipped by frost
I must praise now, for when the short days come
what memories will in secret keep me warm?
I admit, pressed to acknowledge soil and root,
that all I've given I brought with me from home.
I can't deny the tree that bore the fruit.

The Hungarian original of this poem won the Salvatore Quasimodo Prize of Balatonfüred (1993) and the Italian translation the Ada Negri Prize of Lodi (1995).